JEAN THIRIART

THE GREAT NATION

Unitarian Europe – from Brest to Bucharest

translated by

ALEXANDER JACOB

MANTICORE PRESS

The Great Nation: Unitarian Europe – From Brest To Bucharest

Jean Thiriart
Translated by Alexander Jacob
© Manticore Press, 2018

Thema Classification:
JPA (Political Science & Theory), JPFN (Nationalism)

978-0-6482996-8-4

MANTICORE PRESS
WWW.MANTICORE.PRESS

CONTENTS

PREFACE

ALEXANDER JACOB

J JEAN THIRIART (1922-92) WAS, without doubt, one of the most significant pioneers of the project of a united Europe that has been espoused by several contemporary European geopolitical thinkers such as, for example, Alain de Benoist, Robert Steuckers, Claudio Mutti and Aleksandr Dugin. Rather like the American political thinker, Francis Parker Yockey (1917-60) before him, Thiriart was one of the first to pivot his entire political project on the precondition of a liberation of Europe from the control of America, which he considered the principal enemy of Europe. And his two works on united, or Unitarian, Europe published in 1964 and 1965 are important manuals for all European national revolutionaries who wish to continue to fight for the independence of Europe – which remains to this day a vassal state of America.

Thiriart was born in Brussels and participated in socialist movements in Belgium such as the Jeune Garde Socialiste and the Union Socialiste Anti-Fasciste. During the Second World War, Thiriart joined the Fichte Bund (part of the Hamburg National-Bolshevik movement of the 1920s) and then the Amis du Grand Reich Allemand, an association composed of elements of the extreme left in Wallonia who were favorable to European collaboration with the Reich. Thiriart's association with this group led to imprisonment in 1944 and a deprivation of civic rights in Belgium until 1959.

Thiriart re-emerged in 1960, during the decolonization of the Congo, by participating in the foundation of the Comité d'Action and de Défense des Belges d'Afrique which became later the **Mouvement d'Action Civique.**

On March 4th 1962 a meeting was organised in Venice whose participants included, besides Thiriart who represented the MAC and Belgium, the Italian Social Movement from Italy, the Socialist Reich Party from Germany, and the Union Movement of Oswald Mosley from Great Britain. In a common declaration, these organizations proclaimed that they wanted to found a "A National European Party, centred on the idea of European unity, which does not accept satellitisation of Western Europe by the USA and does not reject reunification with the territories of the east, from Poland to Bulgaria, through Hungary."

However, the narrow nationalism of the Italians and Germans rapidly broke up the project of a European National Party. The failure of this attempt at a party organization coincided with the defeat of the OAS (Organisation Armée Secrète), which fought for French Algeria during the Algerian War and which Thiriart sympathised with. Thiriart concluded that the only solution was the creation of a Revolutionary European Party, in a common front with parties or countries opposed to the order of Yalta. The MAC was thus transformed in January 1963 into **Jeune Europe**, a European organization that had members in Austria, Germany, Spain, France, Great Britain, Italy, the Netherlands, Portugal, and Switzerland. The new movement was rather different from the customary nationalist movements in Europe. It was very strongly structured, insisted on ideological formation in true schools of leadership and it tried to implement a central syndicate, the Syndicat Communautaire Européen. While Jeune Europe was banned in France on account of its ties to the OAS, it succeeded in recruiting many members in Italy.

The journals of the organisation, first *Jeune Europe* (1963-66), then *La Nation Européenne* (1966-68), also had a considerable audience. There were Italian counterparts, *Europa Combattente* and *La Nazione Europea* (which was edited by Claudio Mutti, the present editor of the journal *Eurasia*) as well. General Perón, in exile in Madrid, declared "I regularly read *La Nation Européenne* and I entirely share its ideas. Not only as regards Europe but also the world."[1]

Apart from numerous articles related to his Europeanist ideas, Thiriart had. already in 1961, written a 'Manifeste à la nation européene' in which he proclaimed his concept of a Communitarian Europe united against the American and Soviet blocs. This manifesto was followed by *Un empire de 400 million d'hommes*, published in 1964,[2] and the present booklet entitled *La Grande Nation: L'Europe unitaire de Brest à Bucarest* published in 1965.[3]

Jeune Europe also aimed at forming European Revolutionary Brigades to start the

---

[1] The February 1969 issue of *Nation Européene* contained the text of a long interview that Thiriart conducted with Juan Perón.

[2] See my English edition, Jean Thiriart, *Europe: An Empire of 400 Million Men*, Dublin: Avatar Éditions, forthcoming 2018.

[3] The present translation follows the edition published by Ars Magna, Nantes, n.d.

armed struggle against the American occupier, and searched for external support in Europe as well as among third-world revolutionaries. Thus contacts were made with Yugoslavia and Romania, Communist China, and Iraq, Egypt, and the Palestinian Resistance.

In April 1968, the publisher of the journal of Jeune Europe, *La Nation Européene,* Gérard Bordes, went to Algeria with a *Mémorandum à l'intention du gouvernement de la République Algérienne* signed by himself and Thiriart, which proposed that "European revolutionary patriots support the formation of special fighters for the future struggle against Israel; technical training of the future action aimed at a struggle against the Americans in Europe; building of an anti-American and anti-Zionist information service for a simultaneous utilization in the Arabian countries and in Europe". However, this Algerian effort proved to be unsuccessful. Nonetheless, the military support of his militants in the Anti-Zionist combat is incontestable since the first European who fell in the struggle against Zionism, in June 1968, Roger Coudroy, was a member of Jeune Europe.

In Autumn 1968, Thiriart travelled to the Middle East at the invitation of the governments of Iraq and Egypt and the Ba'ath Party. He met Nasser during this visit but, under Soviet pressure, the Iraqi government refused to support the idea of a cooperation between Arab nationalists, including the nascent Palestinian ones, and Thiriart's European Revolutionary Brigades.

The lack of the desired financial and material aid to Jeune Europe and its failure to find a firm base for its pan-European operations - as Piedmont had been for the unification of Italy in the middle of the 19th century - was a severe blow to Thiriart's revolutionary ambitions. Further, the fact that, after the crises of decolonisation, Europe benefited from a decade of economic prosperity reduced the prospects of any revolutionary movement. In 1969, disappointed by the relative failure of his movement and the weakness of his external support, Thiriart renounced militant combat.

In the early 80s, Thiriart worked on a book that was never finished: *The Euro-Soviet Empire from Vladivostok to Dublin*. As the title of this book shows, Thiriart's view of the Soviet Union had completely changed. Discarding the old motto "Neither Washington, nor Moscow", Thiriart assumed a new slogan: "With Moscow, against Washington". Thiriart had already expressed his satisfaction with the Soviet military intervention in Prague, denouncing the Zionist plots in the so called "Prague Spring", in an article entitled 'Prague, l'URSS et l'Europe',[4] where he maintained that

> *A Western Europe free from US influence would permit the Soviet Union to assume a role almost antagonist to the USA. A Western Europe allied, or a Western Europe aggregated to the USSR would be the end of the American imperialism [...] If Russians want to separate Europeans from America—and they necessarily have to work for this aim in the long-term—it's necessary they offer us the chance to create a European political organization against the American golden slavery.*

At the time of the collapse of the Soviet Union, in 1991, he supported the creation of the **European National Liberation Front**, which was the successor of Jeune Europe. It was with a delegation of the EFL that he went to Moscow, in 1992, to meet some of the members of the Russian opposition to Boris Yeltsin. Unfortunately, shortly after his return to Belgium. Jean Thiriart died of a heart attack.

*

---

[4]   *La Nation Européenne"*, n. 29, November 1968.

Thiriart left unfinished many theoretical works in which he analysed the necessary evolution of the anti-American combat in the light of the disappearance of the USSR. The present booklet is a fragment of a larger planned work on European nationalism that the author was unable to complete. It constitutes the first two sections of the six that the projected book was to contain –

1.   Political Europe: a Unitarian state

2.   Economic Europe: a Communitarian state

3.   Ethical Europe: a superior will (Europe as a civilizing nation)

4.   The Historical Party: the political priesthood (in the twentieth and twenty first centuries the historical party will play the same role as that played in the past by the dynasties)

5.   The Paths to Power: preparation, realization

6.   Power: origin, significance, greatness and servitude. Morality and philosophy of power

The first six chapters of *La Grande Nation* deal with 'Political Europe' and the remaining with 'Economic Europe'.

In the political part of this work, Thiriart proceeds from the principle that the vast international scope of modern geopolitics demands that great powers be organized in large national units. Europe can combat its two occupiers, America and Russia, only by integrating the continent into a major power bloc. This power bloc will eventually be the first world power since Europe has the unique distinction of being the originator of the culture that the two pseudo-European powers, the USA and the USSR, pretend to propagate.

The problem that Europe faces is that, even though it is a highly developed nation culturally and industrially, it lacks political unity. Political independence depends on an independent defence organization—as opposed to the American controlled NATO—and Europe must develop this along with nuclear arms. The combat against Communism must be undertaken without dependence on the unreliable support of America, which will have to deal with problems of its own empire in places like South America and the Far East.

Economically, Thiriart is opposed to Communist collectivisation as well as to capitalist plutocracy since both are based on the concept of man as *homo economicus*, as a unit of production and profit. The socio-economic pattern of the European Communitarian nation will be focused on the Promethean possibilities of the European individual and support this individualism in such a way that economic independence is guaranteed to it at the same time that licentiousness is curtailed.

The Communitarian society of Thiriart's Europe will be based mainly on the merit of an individual's work and, while it will be egalitarian in the opportunities it offers its citizens, its society will acquire a natural hierarchical structure in accordance with the differing capacities of these citizens.

Free enterprise will be encouraged, for state ownership leads to the incompetence of a social welfare state. However, capitalist enterprise will be adopted only as a means and not as an end, as it is in the USA. No monopolies will be tolerated and economic organisation will be based on considerations of the dimension and nature of the enterprise so that, for example,

1.   in the case of hydro-electric energy, there will be state property and state management

14

2. in the case of an oil-producing territory, there will be state property and private management in the form of state leasing to an industrial group,

3. and in almost all the rest of industry, there will be only private property and private management.

The socialism of communitarian Europe will neither be a parasitical financial plutocracy nor a bureaucratic state socialism. It will be bound to the natural criteria of competition, responsibility, competence and initiative. Since work is the major criterion of value in Communitarian Europe there will be not only a right to work but also an obligation to it. Parasitical speculators will not be tolerated and concentrations of economic power such as monopolies will be prohibited to prevent the danger of their exercising a political influence that they must not possess. Public disclosure of finances will be obligatory for all:

Not only the least communal administration, institution of public order, will have to give the most public disclosure to its management but every commercial enterprise and every individual will be bound to render public the principal elements of their circumstances

Both managers and workers will be equally considered producers according to their contribution to the work involved in an enterprise. Trade unions will be depoliticised and Europeanised. Ownership of property will be transferred from speculators and politicians to producers. Wealth will no longer be a criterion of classes, only individual capacity will be that.

European economic power can no longer be allowed to subsidise American politics through the infiltration of American finance in European industry and European dependence on a foreign currency like the dollar. Europe must begin to utilise a single European currency of its own. Equally urgently it must repurchase all American assets in Europe, with or without penalties for past exploitations. Evidence of activities contrary to the interests of Europe will result in the summary confiscation of these assets.

In terms of international trade, Europe will be nationalist and protectionist. It will not allow the USA to rob it further of the raw materials that are present in its own former colonies. It will not pay American capitalists, and their European partners, for resources that once belonged to Europe and will no longer suffer a further depletion of its financial resources by having to donate aid to third-world countries – whose corruption is sustained by the international capitalist investors and whose resulting poverty is supposed to be alleviated by Europe. Europe will also not depend on Third World immigrants for labour since they lower the wages of the native Europeans and cannot be easily assimilated into European society.

The purging of American finance from western Europe and the de-collectivisation of eastern Europe will facilitate the political reunification of the two separated parts of Europe into a single communitarian socialist nation. This reunification must be accompanied by a new feeling of 'European' nationalism as opposed to the petty nationalisms of the past. European nationalism cannot be developed as an amalgam of numerous petty nationalisms but only through the guidance of a single revolutionary party. The precise process of formation of the European Party through a carefully cultivated elite is described in greater detail in Thiriart's earlier work, *Un Empire*.

One step forward to the creation of the united Europe that Thiriart envisaged was, indeed, the Common Market that was born of the Treaty of Rome in 1957. Though many of the so-called European nationalist groupings of his time mocked this union as a technocratic one with no potential for the unification of the continent, Thiriart saw in it the same potential for a prospective unification of the continent that the Prussian Zollvererin of 1834 had had for the unification of Germany in 1871. The 'economic child' that was given birth to in Rome could, in the near future, grow into a political colossus – once the false socialism and the false democracy of the two occupiers have been removed from the continent.

In all of humanism there is an element of weakness which comes from its repugnance for all fanaticism, from its tolerance, and from its penchant for an indulgent skepticism, in a word, from its natural goodness …

What we would need today is a militant humanism, a humanism that would affirm its virility and which would be convinced that the principle of freedom, of tolerance and of free inquiry does not have the right to be exploited by the shameless fanaticism of its enemies. Has European humanism become incapable of a resurrection?

Thomas Mann, *Achtung, Europa!*, 1937

INTRODUCTION

LÉON QUITTELIER

THIS BOOKLET HAS a double purpose: it is first of all destined to make the public aware of certain of our fundamental positions; it will serve, besides, as a manual of combat for our militants and our members.

We present here a sufficiently large number of problems by giving, for each, the outlines, the orientation if you like, of our solution. Each of the theses of this booklet would merit, we are sure, much more voluminous explanations but our financial 'autonomy' constrains us to a rather Spartan brevity.

The reader will however be able to discern the direction of our action, its spirit and its method. There will remain for him, then, to make a choice, to opt for or against. We are deeply convinced that on this choice depends the future of Europe, that is to say, the future of all the European, those of the east as well as those of the west, as free men, as free citizens of a free nation.

*

Everybody speaks of Europe. Everybody has his formula 'to make Europe'. Everybody wants Europe. And yet Europe has not been made. On the contrary: the little that has been constructed is always put into question, if it is not already destroyed.

Why?

Because all the formulas proposed up to the present lack the essential, lack vitality.

One cannot make Europe if one does not believe profoundly in it. And one does not believe in Europe if one does not feel it already as a whole, if one does not experience it today as yesterday we experienced, each of us, our little fatherland. One cannot make Europe without loving it, without respecting it, without being proud of it, without having the courage to bear witness to it before the world, to defend it against its enemies.

One cannot make Europe without arousing a profound European national feeling that is alone capable of surmounting petty nationalism and which alone can give today a meaning and an efficacy to the political action of the Europeans.

The Europe of fatherlands of yesterday, that is a Europe of accords, of pacts, of discussions, that is a Europe that is always challenged.

A national Europe is an abstract construction, a scheme of technocrats, that is the quickest way towards becoming satellites and subordination to the big foreign blocs which are vigorously nationalists, implacably imperialists.

*

Europe, this 'pearl' 'has imprudently yielded its impetus to the masses', said Paul Valéry already in 1919.

Oh well! Since it is so, it is important that we Europeans too form a mass. It is for us a question of life or death. The formula that we bring forward—the European Communitarian Party— is the only one that can cause all Europeans to become clearly aware of their solidarity of destiny. The community of destiny calls forth the community of design. And it is this future in common which is the foundation of European nationalism, as it is the foundation of the European Communitarian Party.

Yesterday, the nations were fashioned by the will of the sovereigns.

The modern nations are the work of parties, but of historical parties rather than of political parties.

To fulfil this historical mission, our party responds to three basic conditions:

1.   It is a Great European aggregate: it is directed to all of Europe, not only to western Europe and it can welcome all 'political opinions' insofar as these opinions are not inspired by one of the two foreign powers that occupy Europe.

2.   It is supranational: the party has, for us, priority over the little nation that gave us birth because, for us, the party is Europe and, in serving Europe first, we are conscious of better serving our little fatherland.

3.   It is, finally, revolutionary because it proposes new structures of society, new structures necessary if one really wishes to reunite, one day, into a single nation, into a single state, our Europe today cut into two and subject to opposed political systems.

The European Communitarian Party is from now on the legitimate Europe because the interest of Europe is, for it, the supreme law. The party is already the European nation.

That is why, tomorrow, when all the false prophets and the sorcerer's apprentices will have been unmasked, when Europe will perhaps despair of itself, it is from the European Communitarian Party that the men who finally make Europe will quite naturally emerge.

September 1965

IN GRATITUDE

WITH THANKS TO the men who encouraged and helped me, who were engaged by my side in this Titanic struggle engendered by the challenge that we have posed: to make Europe.

They are already too numerous for me to be able to cite all of them. However, I must give some name of men who have distinguished themselves by their loyalty with regard to me.

In France, these are Gérard Bordes and Francis Thill. In Italy, Pierfranco Bruschi, Massimo Costanzo, Claudio Mutti, Claudio Maranelli, Claudio Orsi, Lucio Martelli, Renato Cinquemani; in Spain, Pedro Valles; in Portugal, Joaquim Rafael Duarte and Léon Quittelier.

Could I ever forget that friend who, finding me in a period of moral trial and knowing that I am not Christian, told me, 'I prayed for you'.

An exceptional mention should be made of my wife, Alice Thyssens, my collaborator at all times.

Finally, my two grown-up children will forgive me for having deliberately sacrificed an important social position in favour of an ideal whose importance they cannot yet measure. My wife, my mother and my children will forgive me also for having deprived them often of the marks of affection that I owed to them as a husband, son and father.

Jean Thiriart

October, 1965

PREFATORY NOTE

IN MARCH 1062, a stay in prison, the third in my political life, had given me the idea and the time to sketch the plan of my first book. In Spring 1964 I published it under the title of *Europe: An Empire of 400 million men*.

At the present moment I possess hundreds of notes on paper which would allow me to easily write a second work, *European Nationalism*.

But I lack time: I am bound by the servitudes of social life on the one hand and of direct political action on the other.

The present booklet is in fact constituted of the summarized and condensed first two chapters of a book which will contain six of them, which are:

1. Political Europe: a Unitarian[5] state

2. Economic Europe: a Communitarian state

---

[5]   Thiriart uses the term 'unitaire' for a Europe considered as a single political unit.

3. Ethical Europe: a superior will (Europe as a civilizing nation)

4. The Historical Party: the political priesthood (in the twentieth and twenty first centuries the historical party will play the same role as that played in the past by the dynasties)

5. The Paths to Power: preparation, realization

6. Power: origin, significance, greatness and servitude. Morality and philosophy of power

With much luck this work could be finished towards the end of 1966.

My life is a double one: I am at some moments on the street, that is then the life of engaged political combat, at other moments I am at the window and watch the world go by.

It is in the rare moments that I am at the window that I write, that I describe –

Jean Thiriart,

September 1965

I – DEFINITION AND MISSION

1. EUROPE, A NATURAL AND NECESSARY WHOLE

POLITICS BEING ESSENTIALLY a relation, a balance, of forces, **there is, at the present moment, no longer any real independence or progress possible except for large political entities** organized on the level of continents.

All politics that is confined in a narrower scope is bound to failure through lack of means. This is true not only from the economic point of view but also from the social, military, cultural, etc. points of view.

Now, the organization of society depends first of all on politics. Politics has priority over economics. The large political entities **must correspond to the natural, geographical, historical, cultural, etc. affinities**, of the people that compose them, otherwise they will remain unstable and carry in themselves the seeds of their collapse.

International balance is conditioned by the formation of these large natural political entities two of which, the USA and the USSR, have already acquired their definitive form and two others of which are in gestation: China and Europe.

A balance of two: USA-USSR is the most dangerous that there can be, particularly for the Europeans who serve as a buffer between these two blocs. The formation of the Chinese entity is, besides, a proof of this: it has acted as a powerful factor of international stabilization by obliging notably the USSR to defend itself on two fronts instead on of one. Europe possesses to the highest degree all the characteristics of **a natural entity and, given its high degree of culture and civilization, given also its privileged central geographical position**, it is, more than any other entity, designed to be **the principal factor of balance for the world and a condition of survival for the Europeans**.

2. EUROPE AS A NATION: A SHARED FUTURE

Europeans possess a very important **shared past**. This past is nothing in comparison with the gigantic shared future that awaits them.

For us a nation is, above all, a **community of destiny**.

Originally a nation is not an ethnic or linguistic entity. What constitutes the reality and vitality of the nation is the **unity of its historic destiny**.

When men, peoples have arrived at almost identical levels of maturity, when a culture is common to them, when geography makes immediate neighbours of them, and the same dangers and the same enemies threaten them, the conditions are given for making a nation.

For us **nationalism is the identity of destiny desired in light of a great shared plan**.

3. EUROPE: THE FIRST WORLD POWER

The third international power in the order of appearance, Europe will be the first in the order of power. This supremacy is inscribed in the statistics:

In population the USSR represents 225 million men, the USA 179 million men, unitarian Europe 468 million!

Thus Europe in itself is more important than the USA and the USSR put together.

At present torn apart by the military and financial occupations of the USSR and the USA, Europe includes: west of the Iron Curtain, 364 million inhabitants, east of it 104 million inhabitants. In western Europe, in other words, in American Europe, the Common Market includes in itself 175 million men. Thus the 'little' Common Market is already the equivalent of the entire USA.

In industrial power Europe surpasses the USSR in all fields; and it is equal or superior to the USA.

As regards the cultural level, it would be too easy to establish comparisons: in geometry, mathematics, music, etc. it is the European culture that gave the entire world a civilization that it is avid to copy.

4. THE MISSION OF EUROPE: THE PILOT NATION

Europe constitutes, in power, the most important natural entity not only **in numbers** (exception being made of China) but also **in quality**.

A miracle of history, Europe, through the **prodigious fecundity** of its culture, created civilization. Now, this culture, the privilege of Europe, is the sign of its fundamental superiority to the USA and the USSR, which retain only the civilization born of our culture.

Every civilization cut off from culture, its root, is sterile, scelerotic and tends to return slowly to barbarism, even if this barbarism is constituted of dollars.

Now, European culture risks being choked if Europe continues to be dominated politically by foreigners.

Only independence can guarantee the conservation of a culture on which the destiny of man depends. For, the destiny of man also depends on the future of Europe, and nothing is capable of taking the place of Europe in this humanist mission. The mission of Europe is to be the Pilot Nation.

II – THE ENEMIES OF EUROPE

WE SHALL NEVER recognize the division of our European fatherland at Yalta in 1945 between the Yankee plutocracy and the Russian Communism.

The perspective of history allows us only today to understand that the European civil war of 1939-1945 was capitalized on by the foreigners in order to reduce the whole of Europe to their mercy and to grab without encountering any opposition all its overseas empires.

The war begun in 1939 did not therefore end in 1945 with the crushing of Hitlerian Germany. In fact, **the Yalta accord inaugurated a new war and this war, directed against the whole of Europe, ended in 1962** with the loss of Algeria.

34

Immediately exploiting our weakness at the end of a civil war, our 'liberators' became our exploiters.

Not only did Russians and Americans appropriate each a half of Europe but, further, the USA ousted Europe from the world, country by country: Italy from Africa, the Netherlands from Indonesia, England and France from Asia and Africa, Belgium from Africa. The USA did that not to 'liberate' the colonized peoples but to take our place and to benefit from our advantages. The fact that they lost what they robbed from us does not diminish in the least their responsibilities. Everywhere that Communism took the place of Europe it is the noxious American politics that we owe it to. Besides, the 'generous' America entered the war in 1941 only at the moment that it was attacked directly by Japan. Before that there was no question at all for it to 'liberate' Europe or of a crusade against Communism.

That is why to join the USA out of concern for defence, as the 'Atlanticists' do, is a mental aberration neighbouring on treason.

As for the USSR, it does not even take the trouble to disguise its imperialistic aims which make use of the Communist ideology as a façade.

6. WE DO NOT WISH TO BE A BOOTY NATION NOR A BATTLEFIELD NATION

The borders of Europe have been **fixed by its history**. They have been implicitly recognized and **authenticated by the foreigners themselves** when, at Yalta, the USSR and the USA divided it into two, each reserving for itself its zone of influence.

From Brest[6] to Bucharest, our torn Europe includes more than 400 million inhabitants whose historical **solidarity** today finds an anguishing confirmation in the **solidarity of destiny which binds them indissolubly**, in spite of the curtains and walls. The solidarity of the past meets the solidarity of the future.

It is within this natural scope that our political action should flourish, and **our first objective is to efface Yalta**.

In the longer term the border of Europe will doubtless extend to Vladivostock, for we think that the instinct of conservation will finally override the ideologies and that, on that day, Russia will need Europeans to contain the Yellow swamp.

While waiting for this, Europe is a booty nation divided between two imperialisms.

---

[6] Brest is a port city in Brittany.

This situation creates a mortal danger for the Europeans: now in a satellite position, the USSR and the USA deliberately hinder our development through a meticulous control or by infiltration, in order to take possession of the first achievements of the small Europe of the Six.[7]

The Europeans are no longer free: their action is limited to the will and the interest of their masters. On the one hand, **it is the brutal stranglehold supported by the tanks of the Red Army (Budapest)**[8], on the other, **it is the slow and crushing economic stranglehold based on the dollar**. They are attempting to suffocate the embryonic Europe. Already.

That is not all: in case of conflict between the two imperialist powers, Europe will be transformed immediately into a battlefield nation. For, finally, it is Europe—or what remains of it—that will defray the costs of an armed confrontation between the USA and the USSR, the two adversaries being in agreement about saving themselves the horrors of nuclearisation.

---

[7] The 'Six' were the six European countries–Belgium, France, Italy, Luxembourg, Netherlands and Germany–that were founding members of the European Communities, which first came into being on the signing of the Treaty of Paris–which established the European Coal and Steel Community–in 1951.

[8] The Hungarian Revolution of 1956 was a national revolt against the Soviet-imposed government of the Hungarian People's Republic.

Booty today, a battlefield tomorrow, that is the fate of Europe if it delays thinking about itself.

7. INDEPENDENT EUROPE: AGAINST NATO

Real political independence does not exist without a force capable of making others respect it. The USA and the USSR have a politics quite entirely based on their nuclear armaments (cf. the Cuba affair).

In order to be really independent Europe **must be capable of making others respect it**, in the same way as the USA, Russia or China are.

Europe must therefore **have its own nuclear force**. Independence is, for the Europeans, the only true guarantee of progress, development, welfare, security, in the long term.

It is absurd to say **that nuclear armaments cost too much**; first, because the means that Europe has are as important as those of the other blocs and, then, and especially, because in the short term the fact of not having the means to make others respect us would cost us more—and then definitively—than the expenses of nuclear armament.

Besides, the European powers contribute, in great measure, to the financial resources of

NATO. The humiliating paradox is, thus, that it is with our money that we procure for the USA a super-army, NATO. What we pay NATO is in reality what we pay to the American army of occupation.

To trust in the USA for our defence is for the true Europeans a position unsustainable in principle and dangerous in fact.

Unsustainable in principle because **that is the same as validating the division of Europe, the USA being the defenders of western Europe alone, their zone of influence**. Dangerous in fact because it increasingly appears that **the USA is losing its impetus everywhere in the world**. The American hypercapitalism is always in danger of an economic catastrophe. Besides, in the years to come, the USA is going to be preoccupied with a series of extremely thorny problems both in South America and in the Far East, two regions which are, for them, infinitely more interesting than a Europe that is a competitor in power.

The USA can thus be transformed suddenly into a very unreliable ally because their vital interests are not in Europe.

NATO, such as it is organized, is totally in the hands of the Americans. One cannot therefore speak of allies, since the relations that exist at NATO between the USA and the European member countries are those of master and subjects.

Europe must therefore form **its own defence organization and, with that, negotiate the alliances that will serve its interests**.

8. INDEPENDENT EUROPE: AGAINST COMMUNISM

Russian Communism occupies our eastern territory and it is deeply infiltrated, in the west, by the diverse Communist parties, especially in Italy and France.

Our attitude on this principal problem must be dictated **by the superior interest of Europe, which includes 100 million Europeans directly subject to the USSR. On the level of principles**, we are the sworn enemies of the Communist ideology which reduces the individual to the role of a blind mechanic. The postulate of the class struggle, the purely materialistic conception of the world, are for us totally false theories overtaken by science as well as by facts but whose noxiousness remains extremely virulent in the masses thanks to the mysticism of the 'Communist paradise' which misleads minds by warping the direction of the natural tendencies of man towards happiness, peace, etc. Consequently, the Communist ideology must be combated through all means. It is the enemy number one.

The political parties which exploit this ideology must be suppressed, so much more because these parties work openly for imperialisms that are foreign to Europe: the Russian and Chinese imperialisms. The Communist parties are therefore intrinsically harmful and politically treasonous to Europe.

The peaceful co-existence of Europe with the USSR cannot be conceived without the preliminary destruction of the Communist parties in Europe. The USSR similarly could not accept to co-exist peacefully with a neighbor that would maintain a political party within it.

As regards the USSR itself, its internal regime does not concern us. From the European point of view we could even hope that Communism may continue **to weaken, in spite of appearances, a neighbouring bloc of Europe**.

9. UTOPIAN GLOBALIZATION: THE UNITED NATIONS AND COMPANY

Political action, in order to be effective, cannot be dispersed in a utopian globalization (the USA).

Globalisation is the expression of the out-of-date conceptions of **the bourgeois-liberal ideology** and of its derivatives which consider that, men being equal, it is possible **to establish general rules applicable to everybody at all times**.

The same internationalism characterizes **the Communist ideology**, first cousin of the liberal ideology. These two ideologies are in fact built on the postulate of a '*homo economicus*', both interested in man as a first cause.

Their most typical representatives are precisely the enemies of Europe: Capitalism and Communism, incarnated in the USA, on the one hand, and in the USSR and China, on the other.

It is hardly necessary to say that the civilization of the USA is totally based on material profit: they are proud of it. As for Communism, the axiom of class struggle is nothing but that of the struggle of the not wealthy to possess the goods of the wealthy.

It is therefore not surprising that these two apparently opposed ideologies, Liberalism and Communism, can agree with each other so perfectly and complement each other in a way.

They have the same roots.

The United Nations is the insurance company of the Globalists.

Europe should therefore withdraw from the United Nations insofar as this organism aims at decreeing universal political rules. The internal affairs of Europe will be regulated by the Europeans, without tutelage of any sort, and by virtue of rules which they will decide themselves to apply amongst themselves according to circumstances. That is what the USA and the USSR do, besides.

Since 1945, the United Nations has been successively a mask, an instrument of American and Russian policies or a theatre for the underdeveloped.

Like its older sister, the League of Nations, which disappeared in a general indifference, the United Nations will disappear in contempt. Already this temple of imposture presents cracks. We should accelerate the collapse by withdrawing as a bloc from this anti-European enterprise.

10. AGAINST MERCENARY DEMOCRACY, FOR A NATIONAL DEMOCRACY

The rule of parliamentary democracy, in a society with capitalist structures like western

Europe, leads inevitably to **the disguised reign of plutocracy.** Money is the common denominator: it permits one to achieve everything, including political power.

This democracy of parties is not true democracy. It is the political replica of finance capitalism.

For more than 20 years it has been offering in western Europe **a shameful spectacle:** sinecures, corruptions, scandals, frauds and impotence.

Its divorce from the nation is complete, it is despised by all, and in the first place by the workers. In it all the powers are concentrated in the hands of a caste of professional politicians cut off from the people and manipulated by financial groups who are often foreigners to Europe.

This democracy is **incapable of making Europe, as it has been incapable of defending it for more than 20 years.**

Furthermore, its internal divisions–the typical democratic fragmentations–always allow Communism or the USA to find allies among those very people who claim to work for Europe.

Europe will not be able to constitute itself through the projection on a larger scale of the defects of the present western regimes.

A radical transformation of our political and social structures is therefore necessary.

In the first place, we want a **European national democracy**, the nation being the communion of the people as a whole. The division into social classes provoked by finance capitalism, repeated by Communism and carefully maintained by the first as well as by the second will be eliminated. **Our democracy will be direct, hierarchical, living, throwing its roots into the entire nation**. It will have **two basic rules**: competence in appointment, responsibility in power.

We reject a Europe governed by legally irresponsible persons and by manifestly incompetent persons.

Our **hierarchy will be that of work, the latter being the criterion of value**.

11. PLUTOCRACY IS INCAPABLE OF DEFENDING EUROPE

If there is a myth to be destroyed it is that of the capacity of the plutocracy which calls itself 'democracy' to defend itself against Communism.

Incapable yesterday of defending itself against Fascism without resorting to another fascism — Communism as it happens—plutodemocracy is essentially an absence of a determination to combat. Where it is necessary to combat it purchases. It purchases peace by selling bits of territory. It calls that 'gaining time', or even 'political negotiations'.

In Africa, in South America, in Asia, the American plutocracy does not succeed in containing Communism in spite of the torrents and monsoons of dollars.

Here, in western Europe, this same plutocracy carefully avoids every direct confrontation with Communism. It plays for time or, rather, it thinks it is playing for time. In fact it allows a huge apparatus of Communist subversion to establish itself in the interior itself of our state structures (the press, education, trade unions). If Communism is a deceptive ideal it does not for that reason exercise any less an unquestionable fascination for the disinherited masses everywhere in the world. Plutocracy has nothing to oppose to this fascination, not even a semblance of idealism. Tomorrow, nobody will want to die for plutocracy. But in its collapse the regime that corrupts Europe should not drag Europe itself down.

To the men misled by the deceptive idealism of Communism, by the bloody imposture of Marxism we should oppose men inspired and united by an authentic ideal. The possibility of defending Europe goes via the destruction of our plutocratic structures which debilitate it and cause it to degenerate.

12. FROM THE IRON CURTAIN TO THE CORDON SANITAIRE[9]

The iron Curtain which cuts Europe into two is the consequence of the division of Europe at Yalta, in 1945, between the USA and the USSR. It would be inaccurate to attribute the responsibility for it to the USSR alone. Let us note in passing the cowardice of the western democracies which, entering into war in 1939 to render justice to Poland, delivered this same Poland, in 1945, to Russia.

We fight with all our strength for the reunification of our European fatherland, from Brest to Bucharest. The destruction, by no matter what means, of the psychological Iron Curtain which divides Europe is one our principal objectives, if not the first.

---

[9] A cordon sanitaire, or sanitary cordon formed of a series of political alliances, was established after the First World War by the French Prime Minister, Georges Clemenceau, in order to stop the spread of Communism into western Europe. It not only sealed off Russia but also surrounded Germany, which was considered a diseased nation.

We should denounce here the partisans of **a rump Europe**, that is to say, of Europe from Bonn to Lisbon. This rump Europe suits very well the plutocratic interests which do not wish to make the Iron Curtain disappear. For them the Iron Curtain is also a **cordon sanitaire**. Knowing well that they will never be able to reestablish the plutocratic structures in eastern Europe, the reactionaries and conservatives prefer to abandon, isolate it, in order to conserve their profits in one part of Europe. The thesis of the plutocratic clique is to conserve its privileges in one part of Europe rather than to establish the unity of **Greater Europe** by sacrificing a part of their interests. We denounce the hypocrisy of the pro-American pseudo-Europeans.

Whereas we wish for an empire from Brest to Bucharest, they wish for a plutocratic republic from Frankfurt to San Francisco.

The passion of the capitalist profits obliterates the sense of national honour, and for us **the fact of the nation** prevails over every other preoccupation.

III – THE POLITICAL GEOMETRY OF EUROPE

13. THE MINIMUM DIMENSION FOR A VIABLE NATIONALISM

THE NATION CAN be born in a viable manner only if it attains the minimum dimension, the minimum critical mass relative to an age.

In the seventeenth century, continental France alone was a sufficient dimension to shine and dominate; from the end of the nineteenth century, France had to necessarily become colonial in order to remain **in the first rank of nations**.

Today, if France is returned to its borders of the seventeenth century, it is a state of second rank. This remark is valid for England, Germany, Italy and Spain.

The notion of **minimum dimension** varies through time.

In the twelfth century, we were powerful, respected and independent at the level of the Duchy of Brittany, in the nineteenth, at the level of colonial France. Today, the European dimension is the **minimum** indispensable for independence. Patriotism finds part of its strength in the emotional realm, but in its superior forms it seeks its bases in the intellectual. Nationalism should be a reasoned passion, a mission of intelligence.

To attach oneself to an old and **non-viable** petty nationalism is a form of sentimentalism. Of suicidal sentimentalism.

We wish for a nationalism of the dimension of the present time, we wish for a viable nationalism: European nationalism.

14. ONLY LARGE NATIONS ARE INDEPENDENT

There are no really independent small nations, that is a law of political physics. To escape the sway of the imperialistic will of a great **power** the small nation will solicit the aid of another imperialist nation. At that very moment it will fall into the servitude that it wished to avoid.

There are brutal and gross servitudes, such as those born of the Russian imperialism, they are visible, explicit. There are others which are more hypocritical, more sly but not less humiliating, such as those born of the American imperialism; they are invisible to the man who is not aware of political and historical matters.

Certain heads of state, certain nations play to themselves a drama of independence. This drama, very precarious besides, only serves to mask the deep fracture that reigns in their own country where the partisans of foreign imperialism watch one other while waiting to fight one other.

Between nations there is no other morality than force, between nations there is no other language than power. Woe to the person who does not hold power. Power is found notably in dimension.

For us the solution here is imperative: Europe.

Those who refuse to be European accept directly or indirectly being Russian or American. It is no longer possible to be German or French today because there is no longer a viable Germany or a viable France.

Freedom is power. Power is dimension.

15. NO MORE DIVISIONS BETWEEN EUROPEANS, THE PAST IS DEAD

More than 100 million Europeans lived through the Fascist and Hitlerian regimes. It is absurd to pretend that the majority of them were opposed to them. It is also equally absurd to deny that these regimes realized, in more than one domain, particularly in the social domain, remarkable works.

But Fascism and Hitlerism were born of particular circumstances in an age which belongs to the past. Every polemics on this subject is not only vain – neither Fascism nor Hitlerism will be reconstituted – but it is harmful, for it maintains or revives resentment between citizens of the same nation. This is what the Communists have well understood in the systematic exploitation that they undertake of the words Fascists, Nazi, etc.

For us, **Europe will be formed both with the former Fascists and with the former Communists, insofar as as they surmount outdated Fascism and Communism.**

16. OUR POLITICAL GEOMETRY: NEITHER RIGHT NOR LEFT

We represent there the thought of the great Ortega y Gasset[10] who says that to be of the Left or of the Right is to choose one of the innumerable modes that are offered to man to be an idiot: both are in fact forms of moral hemiplegia. Unitarian Europe will be formed with people who will have the intelligence to leave the Left or the Right and in no case with people of the Left or people of the Right, stereotypes frozen in their manias and their rites.

To wish for a Europe of the Left or a Europe of the Right is to sabotage Europe knowingly or stupidly.

For one who wishes to situate us in the political geometry, let him consider us as the avant-garde of the Centre, one who unites and integrates the power of dynamism and the wisdom of balance.

17. FOR A NEW AND LOGICAL DISTRIBUTION OF POLITICAL PARTIES

The linear division of the political world going from an extreme Left to an extreme Right is totally overtaken by reality.

---

[10] José Ortega y Gasset (1883-1955) was a Spanish philosopher who focused on the reality of the life of the individual within his historical context.

All the present political activities in Europe should be condensed into three principal groups which are:

1.   The parties of the foreigner, with the American party on the one hand and the Russian party on the other

2.   The archaic or prehistoric parties, those of fierce petty nationalists

3.   The party of the Europeans

In the American party one finds in a jumble the worst reactionary clique of the extreme Right and the most whining mob of the Left.

Thus, in France, Tixier[11] and Guy Mollet,[12] in Belgium the Baron de Launoit[13] and the secretary of the governmental socialist trade unions, are in the same American gallery. All those should be

---

[11]   Adrien Tixier (1893-1946) was a French politician who served as Minister of the Interior in General de Gaulle's Provisional Government of the French from 1944 to 1946.

[12]   Guy Mollet (1905-1975) was the leader of the French section of the First Workers' International from 1946 to 1969 and French Prime Minister from 1956 to 1957, during the Algerian War.

[13]   Paul Auguste Cyril de Launoit (1891-1981) was a Belgian industrialist and financier who was a close friend of Queen Elisabeth of Belgium.

denounced and combated. One should combat the collaborators of the Right or of the Left, for before being of the Right or the Left they are collaborators of the occupier.

By contrast, there are men who, coming from the Left and abjuring its clichés are sincere Europeans; there are men who, coming from the Right and rejecting its manias are sincere Europeans. These men should come together.

18. AGAINST ALL RACISM OF POLITICAL USAGE

It is vain to deny the existence of several races of men, just as it is vain to pretend that these races are equal, **in fact, at the present time**. Similarly, men are not equal in fact: inequality is the human condition itself. But these affirmations, if they have—whether one wishes or not—an influence on politics, **cannot in any case serve as a starting point of a political doctrine**.

We are therefore, in political terms, deeply antiracist and we reprove all racism. The affirmation of the existence of races and their differences is a fact that belongs to ethnological science. The blind people of the Left who try awkwardly to deny these differences and the blind people of the Right who wish to derive a political philosophy from them are, both, judgemental; they have abandoned reality for vows, whether these are pious vows or wicked vows. And politics should be a reality.

Racism and antiracism: two false problems that do not interest us. It is the **political necessities of the defence of Europe** that imposes on us the rejection of all extra-European immigration, whether it is a matter of Blacks, Arabs or Americans (Whites). Besides, the appearance of colour racism to supplant the White race, a will explicity admitted even by the Marxists of Peking, brings about, on our part, an attitude of **legitimate defence**.

Europe, in any case, does not need racism to justify its cultural and historical superiority.

The antiracism of the progressives of our day is nothing but a mechanism destined to dismantle Europe and create, in naïve minds, a guilt-complex followed by political masochism.

19. THE EUROPEAN CONDENSATION: DENSITY OF ACCUMULATED POWER

Europe has been constrained, by the course of affairs, to fall back on itself. Each of its parts has successively lost its colonial empire.

Everything ended in 1962 with the loss of Algeria. This is a turning point in the history of Europe as a nation.

Whereas in the past the European power and lifeblood was scattered, dispersed throughout the globe, today all this strength is condensed in Europe itself. Paradoxically, the loss of our colonies will have been a good thing indirectly and in the long term.

This falling back on ourselves leads us to a recognition.

Thirty years ago Casablanca was politically closer to Paris than Frankfurt was from Nancy. Thirty years ago Matadi[14] was closer to Antwerp than Antwerp was from Düsseldorf. All that has changed. Before 1940, Europe resembled a house with multiple apartments where each had a door to the street, but where there was no door inside. Our doors towards the exterior, towards Africa and Asia, having been walled off, we have been forced to pierce new ones between European provinces.

The few hundreds of thousands of European men that we sent to India, the Near East, to Africa, to Asia, are now available on site, in Europe. This is a favourable condition: the density of European power has gained thereby.

---

[14] The chief sea port of the former Belgian Congo and present Democratic Republic of the Congo.

At the same time, the United States is scattered and wears itself out throughout the world.

20. THE FREEDOM OF THE CITIZEN IS DIRECTLY PROPORTIONAL TO THE POWER OF HIS FATHERLAND

The **citizen** of a large nation is freer than the citizen of a small nation. Each citizen participates in the power of his fatherland, thus in the independence and freedom of the latter.

Conversely, he participates in the dependence and humiliation of his country.

We wish for a powerful fatherland, Europe, for we wish to be free men.

We wish for a powerful fatherland because we wish to be just men: here again social justice is conditioned imperatively by the real independence of our fatherland.

A country which is politically dependent is economically dependent: it is illusory and ridiculous to pretend to be able to make real socialism succeed in any country of Europe as long as the latter is under foreign political tutelage. It is stupid to envisage a socialism in western Europe as long as the latter is under the politico-military occupation of the plutocratic nation par excellence: the United States.

Wishing to be just men, wishing to be free men, we wish a powerful nation through which we will realise our ideals. Each of us will be what Europe will be.

IV – THE ILLUSORY EUROPES

21. NO ORDERLY DIPLOMACY IS DISPERSED

IT IS NOT only stupid but criminal to tolerate diplomatic, military and economic arrangements between ONE of the European countries and an external power, in America, in Asia or in Africa.

Any negotiation between a part of Europe and a power external to it weakens us. A Spanish/American military arrangement, a English/Russian economic accord, a German/American political arrangement are so many treasons with regard to Europe.

Our enemies know and they encourage these games. The USA deals, deliberately, individually with each of the parts of Europe. It is all to their profit.

Europe—even before the creation of the European state—must present itself, in whatever dialogue it may be, as a total, entire Europe. It is an axiom, an imperative of its politics. Our enemies in Washington and Moscow speculate on the somersaults of petty nationalist egoism. We have here once more the proof that petty nationalisms constitute the divisive game of our enemies.

The enemies of Europe have an overall negative policy that concerns the whole of Europe. They are paradoxically more 'European' than the narrow nationalists who, incapable of surpassing their attachment to the native soil, think that they are able to deal as equals with the existing large blocs. What is a European country before the USA or the USSR? **The narrow nationalisms are the best arm used against Europe by the USA and the USSR.**

One exploits the anti-German resentment, the French nationalism, the Spanish dictatorship, etc. One even arouses, when possible, divisions within European nations: for example, the support given by the Communists to every separatist movement.

This nationalist obstinacy **has cost Europe all its colonial empires.**

22. THE SIMPLE ADDITION OF PETTY NATIONALISMS CANNOT ENGENDER EUROPEAN NATIONALISM

Just as Christianity is not the sum of diverse paganisms, the collection of skimpy nationalisms will never give birth to European nationalism.

The old nationalisms should be used not as forms but as a material.

They should be sent to the crucible to be melted and then laminated anew in order to make a unique homogeneous piece.

Those who would oppose this recasting will be cast away, for, like Communism, they constitute a disintegrating element of the European homogeneity.

Historically, the petty nationalisms disappeared at the same time as our former colonial empires. For example, the loss of Algeria sealed the death of French nationalism. It was relatively reasonable and judicious to be a French nationalist in 1939 when the tricolor flag flew in Saigon, Rabat, Tunis, Beirut, Algiers, Dakar. It is ridiculous to be that still today. French nationalism today is no longer a realism but a nostalgism. The lost dimension beyond the oceans is to be regained on the continent.

23. AGAINST THE EUROPE OF FATHERLANDS, WHICH IS THE EUROPE OF GRANDPA

Europe should be Unitarian. Confederal Europe or a Europe of fatherlands are conceptions whose imprecision and complication hide the lack of sincerity or senility of those who defend them.

Europe should perhaps first go through a brief intermediate stage of federalism. Federal Europe will be the transition between the fatherlands – which is nothing but present Europe – and Unitarian Europe, the Europe of Europeans, irreversible Europe.

In no case can the federal formula be considered as a goal.

The process of the federalist stage followed by Unitarianism will be applied in case of peaceful conditions.

On the contrary, if, through the fact of the opportunities of history, Europe should be born in an armed revolutionary struggle, the passage will be made directly from the present state to the unitarian condition, the party transforming itself naturally into a historical and national Unitarian State.

One must put an end to the petty bourgeois conception of the army separated from politics.

An opposition revolutionary party living at present in a legality which is profitable to it can, tomorrow, be called to form instantaneously the cadres of a Resistance army to a cruel occupier.

If this Resistance emerges victorious from the combat, it is to lead to power and its great achievements, of which the unity of Europe is the very foundation. In this case the federalist intermediary will not exist.

One should point out, on the other hand, that those who are most recalcitrant to European supranationality are in fact the most complacent to the Yankee supranationality.

24. THE PSEUDO-EUROPES

The evidence of Europe is such that even its occupiers are obliged to speak a European language. There are a number of 'European' organisations, committees, circles. Europe is in fashion and nourishes many dilettantes and intellectuals. From this Europe that is spoken of, from this Europe of dining tables will not emerge a Europe of flesh and blood.

This latter will occur when **the faith in Europe as a nation will have penetrated the masses and enthused the youth**, that is to say, when there will be **a European mystique, a European patriotism**.

The true Europe will not be borne by jurists and political party members: it will be the work of combatants who have faith, of **revolutionaries**.

That is why we reject the theoretical Europe, the legal Europe of Strasbourg[15] which has already committed a double treason: it has abandoned eastern Europe to the Communists, it has accepted the total subject of western Europe to Washington.

25. NO NATION WITHOUT NATIONALISM

If Europe, in order to survive and assume its mission in the world, should become unitarian, that is to say, form a single nation, a single state, a single fatherland, it should **suppress the ferments of division** that exist between its citizens, **without for that reason wishing to create a standardized type, standardized against that which the European genius is. Unity in fecund diversity**, such is our objective: in other words, political unification is the only serious guarantee of the conservation of the European diversity.

Subjected to the USA or the USSR, Europe would be really flattened, levelled to the low, either in the Yankee manner or in the Communist manner.

---

[15] Strasbourg, in the Grand Est región of France, is the seat of several European institutions, such as the Council of Europe established in 1949.

One should therefore accept, originally, at the start, the reality of a European nation because there is no nationalism without a nation and no nation without territory. One cannot be a European nationalist if one does not have faith in the reality of Europe, if one places Europe in the category of 'possibilities'.

Every valuable action begins with a faith, not with a 'perhaps'.

A Europe of nations, or of fatherlands, or of states, is impossible because it can be realized only through accords, pacts, treaties, which last for a certain time and perpetuate, through the very fact of their existence, the reality of parties that are distinct and opposed to one another in one way or another. Moreover, how does one harmonise, and who will, a multiplicity of particular pacts?

However, **the patriotic sentiment is a fundamental value which Europe needs**. It is necessary therefore that the narrow nationalists understand that the best way to love their small fatherland and serve it is to love and serve Europe. The sum of diverse particular nationalisms can never produce that great patriotic feeling that is superior and necessary.

A Europe without nationalism is equally impossible. **This is an abstract concept**, typical of the 'breathless' Left, that is a contradiction in terms. What is a nation without a national sentiment?

V – EUROPEAN REALISM

26. NUCLEAR ARMS IN EUROPEAN HANDS ALONE

RUSSIANS AND AMERICANS complement each other admirably to justify the occupations of Europe. The Americans tell us, 'We are here to defend you against the Russians'. To which we reply that we can defend ourselves by ourselves. To which they retort: 'But you do not have the nuclear bomb'. We shall finish by announcing that Europe must possess its own nuclear armaments.

As soon as western Europe possesses its own nuclear armaments there will no longer be any valid pretext for the American occupation.

The same reasoning is maintained in eastern Europe between the European Communist leaders and the Russian leaders of Russian origin.

The same response should be given: nuclear armaments should be entrusted to the European Communist powers under the condition of the departure of the Red Army.

The military denuclearization of Europe that the progressives in the conscious or unconscious service of Moscow wish for is a criminal stupidity. An empty military brings about a historical suicide.

On the contrary, it is the creation of two European nuclear armaments which will constitute, for everybody, the guarantee of balance, first, and of the departure of the occupiers, later.

One does not use a grenade against an enemy who is a metre away, one does not throw an atom bomb against an enemy who is 50 kilometres away. Only a fool could imagine a nuclear war between the two Europes—when one knows the technological details of this type of war!—that would be a mass suicide.

With regard to this situation, why would the Russians or Americans worry about fighting between themselves IN OUR COUNTRY from Bucharest to Paris, in order to avoid bombarding each other in their countries?

For us western Europeans it is less disturbing to know that the bombs are in the hands of the leaders of Prague than in the hands of those of Moscow. And the opposite is also equally true: for the eastern Europeans it is less dangerous to know that the bombs are in the hands of the leaders of the west than in the hands of the Americans. In case of a USA/China conflict, the two Europes temporarily separated would make a simultaneous declaration of absolute neutrality. This is only one—realistic—stage towards the reunification of Europe, in no case a goal.

The dialogue between the two Europes will be infinitely easier once the occupiers have left, willingly or not.

27. THE DOUBLE OCCUPATION, THE DOUBLE TREASON, THE DOUBLE LIBERATION

The invasion of Europe and its occupation in 1944 were simultaneous. After 1945 the occupations were duly concerted between the USA and the USSR.

The liberation of Europe will happen in an equally simultaneous fashion.

It is to give evidence of political naivety to imagine that Russia will leave eastern Europe in a unilateral fashion. **One who wishes the departure of the Russians must wish that of the Americans, and vice-versa**; as regards the collaboration with the occupier, those who sell themselves to the Americans, the 'Atlanticists', are not less contemptible than those who sell themselves to the Russians.

The double liberation of Europe will occur notably through the concerted action of those who in our country in the east wish the departure of the Russians along with those in our country in the west who wish the departure of the Americans.

28. NOT TO CONTRIBUTE TO THE COHESION OF OUR COMMUNIST ENEMIES

We do not have to consolidate Communism by considering it through the lens of an anti-Marxist Manichean, that is to say, by putting Moscow, Peking and Belgrade in a random manner into the same bag.

We should coldly exploit the internal contradictions of the Communist world, that is to say, **treat the different Communists differently**. For example, our economic relations with eastern Europe must be developed in a different climate from that of our relations with the USSR.

If it is reasonable to help, under precise political conditions, eastern Europe, in order to encourage it to emancipate itself from Moscow, it is, on the contrary, absolutely necessary to refrain from reinforcing the Russian industrial apparatus.

One should therefore practise a discrimination in our anti-Communism and offer to the Communist leaders of the east honorable conditions if they wish to reject the Russian tutelage.

In our eyes they are Europeans before being Communists.

If it is in the order of things that the east-west dialogue should take place at the level of the occupying powers of Europe, between Washington and Moscow, it is in the same order logical that the east-west dialogue for the Europeans should take place between us and our captive capitals.

If tomorrow a national Communist regime of eastern Europe feels threatened by an aggressive return of pan-Russian imperialism and casts an appeal for help, the most determined of the anti-Communists of western Europe should respond to it and travel there as volunteers to fight arm in hand. Here the national European fact should outweigh, without a doubt, the repugnance to Communism.

29. THE REFUGEES OF THE EAST: HONORARY CITIZENS OF THE WEST

The refugees of the provinces of eastern Europe are welcomed with more or less 'charity' in the provinces of western Europe.

We demand for our brothers of the east who are refugees to the west immediate European citizenship granting them all civil and political rights in ALL of western Europe.

The refugees from the east are AT HOME here in the west; we cannot tolerate that they be included among 'tolerated foreigners'.

Refugees from the provinces of the east, you are European citizens.

For us Europe is absolutely indivisible; that is the first postulate of our doctrine.

Thus the realistic necessities of the politics that can perhaps lead us to negotiate with the Communists of eastern Europe cannot make us forget, at any time, that our solicitude and our gratitude must go, in the first place, to those who have fought for a non-Communist Europe. The refugees from the east are our brothers; the Communist leaders of eastern Europe are at most possible or necessary interlocutors.

30. PEACE THROUGH THE DIVISION OF THE WORLD. THE BALANCE OF BLOCS

When one speaks of peace one should specify of what peace.

It can be the Sovietic peace, which for many of us would signify the peace of the graveyard; it can be the American peace, that is to say, the peace of gilded slaves, but slaves; it can be the European peace, in independence and freedom. That is the only one that we accept.

We wish for a peace that is an act of intelligence and not a peace that is an act of weakness. We despise violence but we appreciate force, because only force allows one to be peaceful.

When one speaks of peace, one can equally distinguish the ways of achieving it. Peace is engendered through a balance of forces and not through pious wishes.

This balance of forces will be realized for the whole world when the latter is divided between the real powers that are Europe, the United States, Russia and China.

The present international instability derives from the intention that has become ridiculous —it was not that in 1945—of Moscow and

Washington to share the world into two zones of influence. The world divided into two should be substituted with a world divided into four.

VI – THE REALIZATION OF EUROPE

THE COMPLETED FORM, the perfect form, is the nation-state, at once organization and feeling, at once structures and communion of minds.

The technicians of the Common Market prepare an embryo of a European **state**. In no case do they aspire to create a European nation.

The technicians—very valuable in their specialisations—who are irritated at not being able to reduce the old petty nationalisms which slow down the management of Europe, commit a very simple mistake; they wish to supplant a concept of nation with a concept of state, confusing volumes and surfaces.

To put an end to the petty nationalisms one should oppose to them not the cold logic of the

European state but the dynamic warmth of a larger 'European' nationalism.

In Strasbourg, Luxembourg and in Brussels, the technicians prepare with competence a European STATE. But this state will remain an inert, static, construction if one does not breathe into it the historic LIFE that is national feeling.

Europe will not be either a state or a nation. Europe will be both at the same time. It is we who will, definitively, give life to Europe by bringing nationalism to it, as, in the ancient mythology, Aphrodite gave life to the Galatea of Pygmalion.[16]

32. EUROPE: A UNITARIAN REPUBLIC WITH AN IMPERIAL VOCATION

Europe cannot be a sum, a collection of small nations which would be governed separately as feudalisms or particularisms inspired by privileges or by Romanticism.

Europe cannot be a collection of states bound by fear on a temporary basis.

Europe will be one and indivisible. It will be a whole composed of integral parts – its provinces.

---

[16] The story of Pygmalion and Galatea is found in Ovid's *Metamorphoses*.

These parts will not be able to separately have a complete existence because they are not wholes that are simply united but parts forming a single whole.

A Unitarian republic, Europe is constrained to an imperial vocation from the fact of its great size and its superiority.

The empire here is at once a community of culture and a community of destiny.

33. WE ARE THE LEGITIMATE EUROPE

We shall not be contented with a Europe on paper and less with a satellite Europe, a sort of American super-Panama on the one hand, or a provincial annex of Russia on the other.

Without independence there is no nation.

All the Europes imagined up to the present are illusions, for all would collapse instantaneously without the support of a foreigner.

The Europe that we shall make is the Europe of the peoples living on our territory, living, fraternal, real Europe, the legitimate Europe.

Legitimacy belongs to those who fight sincerely for a just cause. Just as in 1956 in Budapest the heroic Hungarian insurgents were the legitimate Hungary, **we are the legitimate Europe**.

34. EUROPE STARTING FROM A HISTORICAL PARTY

To make Europe or, rather, a sort of Europe, many formulas have been tried: the economic formula with its liberal-bourgeois postulate of the *homo economicus*, the formula of parties, states, nations, with its presuppositions and reluctances, etc.

There have equally been the tentatives of a Europe starting from a preponderant nation. These were the tentatives of the French Europe under Bonaparte and of German Europe under Hitler. There is nothing more to return to that and especially nothing to want to return there.

All failed because none present a valid solution to **the principal problem of political unity**.

On the contrary, recent history shows us that a revolutionary team become a revolutionary party and then a **historical party** (that is to say, a party which CREATES the formal nation) can successfully make nations. This was the case of Tunisia with the Néo-Destour,[17] of Morocco with

---

[17]   The Neo Destour, or the New Constitution Liberal Party,

the Istiqlal,[18] of Algeria with the FLN.[19] Every time a revolutionary party. After the seizure of power, this party must remain, for a while, the sole party in order to consolidate the structures of the nation that has just been born. This type of party never hesitates before a resort to arms when their need is felt. It is in this notably that it differs essentially from the divisive parties, the talkative parties that we know in a parliamentary plutodemocracy.

The solution that we propose is the clearest, the most rapid (and it is a matter of urgency to make Europe) is that of the European Party.

This political organization has the same forms as those of the future European state of which it is the prefiguration and microcosm: it is the integrated, hierarchical, centralized European national party. In its womb the best Europeans vivify Europe before the birth of the European state. The party is in some way a pre-state.

---

was a Tunisian political party founded in 1934 by Tunisian nationalists who led the Tunisian independence movement after the Second World War.

[18]   The Istiqlal, or Independence, Party of Morocco was established in 1937 and spearheaded the fight for Morocco's independence from France.

[19]   The Front de Libération Nationale was a socialist party that led the nationalist movement during the Algerian War (1954-1962).

In the image of the state that it is destined to make the European PARTY cannot be an unstable amalgam made in the name of an illusory union: it is an organization of combat conceived in the name of unity. A 'federal' party could not give birth to a Unitarian Europe. The party is thus quite necessarily unitarian, its regional sections being only the parts of a whole and not merely associated entities.

One should denounce the vanity of parties which call themselves European but which are deeply sub-divided by petty nationalisms. There cannot be any question of adding a 'German' European party to a 'French' but indeed of bringing into a single school of thought and action sections of French linguistic expression and sections of German linguistic expression into a single apparatus.

It is a matter of a party which, while being **political** (because it is a matter of organizing the European community) is above all a **historical** party.

That means that all the political tendencies (except the Communists and the pro-Americans) can be integrated into it on condition of accepting at the start, as the supreme law, the interest of Europe envisaged as a unitarian nation, as a common fatherland.

It is not possible to do otherwise, because Europe cannot be made starting with existing and competing political parties: there are attempts to make a Socialist Europe, a Christian Democratic Europe, etc.

Europe will not be the enlarged projection of the defects of the existing regimes.

This party has western Europe **as its initial base**. It is **a single party** because it is the only one of its kind and because it concerns all of Europe (in its objective). And also because it is the only political party capable of encompassing all the others.

This formula of **a single party is indispensable for any revolution**. Now, it is indeed a question of making a revolution.

The objective is worth the trouble: it is a matter, for the Europeans, of life and death. The European party is the party of public salvation of all the Europeans.

VII – PRINCIPLES

35. NEITHER COMMUNISM NOR PLUTOCRACY

EUROPE WILL BE constructed in the struggle against the two materialisms which dominate the world at present: the Communist materialism and the Yankee materialism, the first being that of scarcity, the second that of satiety. These two materialisms, that of the poor as well as that of the rich, leave man unsatisfied and unfulfilled on the spiritual level but also paradoxically on the material level.

These two systems end in the same result: the enslavement of man considered exclusively, in both cases, as a means or an instrument of production.

36. AGAINST THE HYPERTROPHY OF ECONOMIC POWER AND THE CORRUPTION OF POLITICAL POWER

We are for private property when it is the recompense of work and the reward of effort. We are for the ownership of commodities of enjoyment and utility; we are against the ownership of commodities of speculation.

Communitarianism means a maximum of private ownership within the following limits:

10. no abusive exploitation of the work of others

11. no interference in politics through hypertrophy of the concentration of economic power

12. no collaboration with foreign interests in Europe and for the profit of the latter.

When property, through accumulation, comes to constitute a means of interference, an instrument of pressure on political power, one arrives at the condition of a plutocracy, a situation that we reject and which we will break.

Nothing will serve to conceive ideal political systems if the latter are not protected from the temptations and corruptions offered by the concentrations of economic power. **We are against the domination of politics by economics**. With greater reason against the domination of politics by direct or indirect financial corruption. The first measure that is imposed is therefore the destruction of the corrupting power represented by the hypertrophy or the concentration of property.

For us, property is legitimate when it remains a means of enjoyment and illegitimate the moment that it becomes a means of interference into public duty.

37. POLITICS CONTAINS AND DOMINATES ECONOMICS

The power of a nation is measured by the intensity of its foreign policy; it is measured also by the fact that politics concerns the totality of human activities. In a large nation, politics dominates, notably economics and order.

In our plutocratic states the bourgeois ideal is profit. Thus, the economy that procures profit is the goal and the state the means to achieve it. Our states do not have politics but international activities which vary according to the immediate financial interests; one makes war without care in order to come out of an economic depression; one will become the friend of the Black if one can derive a small provisional benefit from it; one will equip a future enemy if one finds some money in that.

A regime that limits itself to procuring benefits for the financiers and consumer-pleasures for the masses is condemned to leave only a fleeting and contemptible trace in history; this regime will not be able to resist adversity when it presents itself. One does not appear at Marathon[20] or a Salamis[21] with armies of consumers.

The European national-communitarian state maintains that politics contains and determines everything that constitutes a truly great nation: an art, a style, a morality, a will to perfection and superiority, the social justice which reinforces the homogeneity of a community, the power which guarantees freedom.

It also maintains that economics is one of the means of the state, one of the means of power of the state.

---

[20] The Battle of Marathon (490 B.C.) was fought between the invading Persians and the citizens of Athens.

[21] In the Battle of Salamis (480 B.C.), the Greek city-states under the general Themistocles defeated the Persian navy of Xerxes.

Consequently, every profit that does not make the state greater is illegitimate and every profit that diminishes it is criminal.

Strong in its political power, the European state will use economics to realise its superior designs.

38. FREE ENTERPRISE A FACTOR OF PROGRESS

We have already examined the political abuses of a certain capitalism. One should avoid extending the condemnation of this capitalism to free enterprise. As much as the first corrupts the political function so much does the second ensure the vitality of economics.

Free enterprise corresponds to natural laws: by permitting competition it ensures selection, by guaranteeing initiative it does not choke emulation, by placing each person before his responsibilities it recognizes values. From the free play of these positive factors is born maximum productivity.

Capitalism knows ONLY productivity without regard for social justice; Marxism, in pursuit of a chimerical or abstract 'class justice', neglects or has neglected the importance of the feeling of freedom in work.

The communitarian mission consists in checking that this maximum productivity is guaranteed by a vigilant social justice.

39. ECONOMIC NATIONALISM A FACTOR OF POLITICAL UNIFICATION

The nation on the path of development—and that is the case of Europe—cannot allow itself total free trade but it should, on the contrary, favour its growth and its political unification through a certain protectionism. Economic nationalism, even in its implicit or unconscious forms, contributes powerfully to the formation of the unitarian political nation.

Thus the economic Zollverein[22] allowed the formation of the Second Reich, that of Bismarck. Thus the Common Market, without its promoters suspecting it, will allow the formation of the European empire.

The Common Market must not be a drainage channel for the American economy but a catalyst of political Europe.

---

[22] The Zollverein was a customs union of German states that was established by Prussia in 1834. It was taken over by the German Empire in 1871.

We do not have to import oranges from California when Spain produces them, nor citrus fruits from Florida that we can find in our country in Bulgaria or in Romania.

The Common Market will be for us an instrument of political penetration into eastern Europe, towards which it should be oriented. Its economic power must serve our designs for the great reunification from Brest to Bucharest.

40. AGAINST UTOPIAN ECONOMICS, AGAINST THE ECONOMICS OF PROFIT, FOR AN ECONOMICS OF POWER

Utopian economics is based on theoretical constructions with moral pretensions. It leads in a straight line to failure or scarcity if it does not sink into ridicule or odium. It is the USSR, an agricultural nation, that has to import cereals twenty years after the end of the war!

The economics of profit is that in which we live. It is the capitalist system. For some short-term profit capitalism will kill the long-term national interests. Thus the English textile mill owners installed their factories in the Orient in order to find low salaries, reducing the English workers to unemployment without the least scruple.

Given the opportunity it will not hesitate to deliver strategic materials or instruments to a foreign nation which will be the enemy tomorrow. If it finds a profit in it that is sufficient for it.

The economics of power aims at the maximum development of the national potential. It will never leave unexploited national resources in order to favour stateless interests; it will never help to reinforce nations that could be enemies tomorrow, it will take care to see that the economy of the nation is, as far as possible, autarkic in the strategic field.

41. NO SOCIALISM WITHOUT A NATION

The Marxist theory tried to deny the existence of the principle of the nation. The facts have contradicted this postulate, and today we witness the spectacle of contradictions within the Communist world. A Chinese national Communism is opposed to the Russian national Communism, after the Yugoslav national Communism detached itself from Moscow.

In Europe, even this evidence has not yet been perceived by the retards of Marxist theory. Also, failing to freely accept the concept of the nation, the Marxists of the Left betray the USSR to the benefit of a foreign power and the Marxists of the Right, the parliamentary socialists, are totally prostituted to the United States.

The Marxists who toil on in Europe in their negation of the nation and in the dream of a utopian globalism have ended up losing all personal character and become satellites themselves to foreign nationalisms.

Where there is no power there is no freedom. Only the first can guarantee the second.

Where there is no nation there is no independence. **The nation is the container and socialism is the content**.

There cannot exist any socialism in the abstract. There is a Yugoslav socialism, a Soviet socialism; but nowhere is there a socialism by itself or a socialism in itself.

Those who attempt this formula end up in foreign subjection. Our parliamentary socialists, by refusing Europe as a nation, end up in the most humiliating dependence on a capitalist foreign power: the USA.

The realization of socialism demands a national habitat.

42. AGAINST THE STERILE CLASS-STRUGGLE

The suppression of the proletariat will be realized by the liberation of the workers. We are fiercely opposed to any social organization based on the struggle of classes within a nation. Communism, like capitalism, which are both constructions on a plan of the class-struggle, each on its side and sometimes in common accord, endeavours to maintain the workers in a situation of material and spiritual inferiority. Communism is the best ally of capitalism and vice-versa. **We will return to the workers their dignity and their responsibilities**. We shall suppress the social classes by giving the place of honour to the work of the individual, the sole criterion of value. Our hierarchy will be based essentially on work. We wish for a dynamic community through a collaboration in the work of all the citizens.

The solidarity among the citizens of the same nation, from the highest technological rank to the unqualified manual labourers, is obvious: a crisis that strikes one strikes the others, a development that favours one favours the others.

That is an effective solidarity. That is national solidarity.

On the contrary, the solidarity between the worker of the Parisian suburbs and the farmer of the Congo is and will remain a figment of the imagination.

VIII – MAN

43. NO INDIVIDUAL POLITICAL FREEDOM WITHOUT PERSONAL ECONOMIC FREEDOM

AN INDIVIDUAL WHOSE accommodation is provided by the state, whose employment is offered by the state, does not have any freedom any more. His proprietor and employer are one and the same anonymous person, thus so much more cruel.

There is no political freedom in a statist collectivist society. Political freedom remains theoretical in a system where the person who wants to claim the use of freedom would see himself punished by social death.

Social death is the proprietor state chasing its tenant, the employer state dismissing its employee, the educationist state prohibiting access to higher education to the children of the person who is a rebel against collectivist conformism.

The security needs of men should not in any case suffocate their libertarian demands.

In a society where the state alone determines or possesses accommodation, employment and the social hierarchy, the repression of freedom is no longer a political fact but a simple administrative measure on the economic level.

An economically dependent man is a man without political freedom.

That is why we consider that we should **tend towards familial proprietorship of housing and to plurality of authority in the work sector.**

44. FROM THE PROLETARIAN TO THE PRODUCER, BY WAY OF THE WORKER: THREE ESTATES, THREE DIGNITIES

In two centuries, between 1800 and 2000, millions of men have passed from the condition of a proletarian to that of a producer.

The proletarian was the exploited man, whose work represented a commodity bought at the lowest price; If his condition was superior to that of the wild beast it was often inferior to that of the domestic animal.

The proletarian has almost disappeared from Europe; that is related to political factors but above all, and principally, to industrial progress. The true proletarian exists now only in the underdeveloped world. He exists still in the Communist phraseology indispensable for subversion or for myth.

The worker represents already a dignity superior to that of the proletarian; his revolt is organized and his life is partially decent.

But if the proletarian was a miserable exploited and unorganized man, **the worker, in spite of his improved material condition, remains manipulated between the hands of the leaders of the pseudo-socialism: the parliamentary socialism**.

The Communist subversion will abundantly use the word proletarian in its vocabulary. The parasites of the parliamentary pseudo-democracy will use and abuse the word worker.

The former look for robots, the latter for an electoral clientele.

We wish first of all for the disappearance of the last proletarians, but also for the transformation of the workers into producers. The worker remains a regimented being carefully placed in barracks to form a docile mass in the service of a parasitical clergy of professionals of governmental syndicalism and of corrupt parliamentarism.

The producer that we wish for will be an accomplished citizen, not only conscious of his rights but also of his duties, a man free in his decisions and responsible for his own future. After having acquired the dignity of the worker over that of the proletarian, man should now acquire the dignity of the producer over that of the worker.

45. FROM THE RIGHT TO WORK TO THE OBLIGATION TO WORK

The society of yesterday included openly a class that did not work and lived very well.

The thing was so normal that it was even considered as honorable to enjoy this condition.

At the same time, at the other end of the scale of social classes, men who had only their work to survive had to struggle to obtain the right to a permanent work that would put an end to the insecurity of intermittent work.

That was the right to work. It is no longer contested by anybody.

The transformation of the European national-communitarian society will be achieved only through the introduction of an obligation to work.

Today, the self-proclaimed man of independent means has given place to the camouflaged parasite.

The community bears a very heavy burden, that of a great variety of non-producers, going from the trade union and political leaders to the state pen-pushers, through the professional 'intellectuals', the fraudsters of finance and of 'popular' credit and the door-to-door salesmen of the advertising-cancer.

In our plutodemocratic societies each real producer works several days a month to fatten the trade union leaders, the parliamentary gossips, the bureaucrats of the state, the unworthy intellectuals, the usurers of finance and the agents of advertising.

The European national-communitarian state will take care to strictly limit these sectors or to suppress some of them to the benefit of the really productive sectors.

To flush out the modern parasite and to put him to work, that is what we mean by obligation to work.

46. EQUALITY OF OPPORTUNITY, GUARANTEE OF SELECTION

As much as egalitarianism, as a principle, is contrary to reality, so much is the equality of opportunity important.

This equality of opportunity is the principle even of the recruitment of the elites.

The vigour of a society derives from the majority and, if possible, the totality of the very gifted or exceptional individuals finding themselves in the apparatus of power.

Education cannot counter-balance the possession of gifts or replace their absence. It is to each generation that the problem of selection is posed. The gifted or exceptional individual does not transmit his gifts: they disappear with him.

All the societies that ignore this law of nature degenerate slowly. By falsifying the criteria of selection through socio-political heredity either in the mercantile bourgeoisie or in the parties in power, by dealing in spinelessness and dishonourable behavior, one weakens the society, one chokes the rise of individuals of value or throws them into the opposition.

What is true of society is true of the state, is true of the party.

The national-communitarian state will take care vigilantly not to go against the natural mechanisms of the appearance and rise of the elite that will be replaced with every generation.

Every particularly capable individual will not encounter any difficulty in rising in the **social** hierarchy. In this regard, free education is one of the basic principles of our social doctrine.

47. AGAINST THE SOCIAL ANT-HILL AND BARRACK, FOR A SOCIALISM DETACHED FROM BUREAUCRACY

The goal pursued by the political leaders is to ensure for itself the control of a docile mass.

For that the 'workers' are duly catalogued, numbered and classified.

We refuse the social ant-hill proposed by these politicians, **we reject the civilization of registration forms**.

It is a sad world from which risk, initiative, personal responsibility have been banned. The individual is crushed, reduced to the rank of a termite or an ant.

What would be the use of suppressing the defects born of the egoism of the liberal society to replace them with the invasive and costly parasitism of the new and abundant political clergy?

Our communitarian socialism will respect the individual, it will destroy these suffocating termites and will implement the natural criteria of a healthy society: **a maximum of competition, a maximum of responsibility and competence**.

IX – APPLICATION – METHODS

48. ACCESS TO PROPERTY: ROOTING MAN IN SOCIETY

THE GOAL FOLLOWED by Communism and its successors is the political and psychological control of the masses through economic regimentation.

In this universe of concentration, the individual sees that he is forbidden access to private property: he must be docile, he must therefore remain a tenant. Our communitarian socialism is determined to destroy all the concentrations of wealth capable of corrupting political power by creating a state within a state.

At the same time, we are determined to give and to favour access to small property to all producers.

The moral fulfilment of man demands that he possess his own hearth, his roof. The ownership of his dwelling is, for almost every man, the symbol of security.

The housing at present rented out by the communal or state collectivities should be systematically sold to all the producers; the present rents slightly raised will then serve to pay, in some years, the purchase of the property.

The stability of families depends in large part on the existence of a fixed home. Nomadism is a factor of the destruction of families.

The stability and the power of a state reside in the multiplicity of small and medium properties.

Each producer, in having access to the property of his family dwelling, will root himself deeply in the society.

The Communist or social-political collectivism wishes to make of each producer a docile tenant; we will make of each producer the legitimate proprietor of his home.

49. REJECTION OF THE 'CARROT AND STICK' FORMULA OR THE PRICE-SALARY RACE

In our plutocratic regimes the complicity between the money powers and the political leaders is illustrated particularly in the farce of the trade union 'struggle'.

The struggle for salary raises has no meaning as long as the problem of prices is not regulated simultaneously, according to the realities.

The farce played out by our social politicians consists in 'snatching' victories from capitalism in the form of salary increases. Some weeks later the prices regain, and often surpass, the salary increases.

Thus the trade union leaders will have acquired prestige among their troops, the producers will have the feeling, the illusion of a victory and the capitalist world will recuperate a little later by raising the sale prices.

We witness here a parody of social progress, a permanent show.

Frequently bosses and trade union leaders, in the most 'advanced' plutocratic nations, organize secretly, together, the strikes and the 'victories of the proletariat'.

The European national-communitarian state will give to the producers the economic accounting of the production, exposing the parasitical sectors, the weak sectors and the abusive 'social' intermediaries.

When the producer knows where the parasites are to be found that live on his work, he will be the first to wish to destroy them.

50. SPECIFIC ORGANISATION AND REGULATION OF THE DIMENSIONAL ECONOMY

A rule: *the superior European national interest*

The groups of particular interests and the chapels of sectarian ideologues must yield to it.

We reject labels: statists, levelers, liberals, capitalists. We are, above all, partisans of a **pragmatic economics**.

Neither systematic dirigisme nor unrestrained liberalism: an organization of the economy subject to the political necessity, but shared as follows:

- National management in the form of direction, for all sectors of strategic importance and for the majority of the activities of the primary sector of the economy (coal, petrol, hydroelectricity …)

- Mixed capital-work management by all the producers without distinction, for several heavy industries of the secondary sector (metallurgy, sheet metal works, chemical works)

- Private management, for light industry, the small enterprises and the distribution and service networks of the tertiary sector as well as for organisations such as clinics.

We distinguish thus three types of management:

a. national management

b. mixed management by all producers

c. private management

They constitute the three principal forms of the specific organization of the European national communitarian economy.

On the other hand, we perceive the necessity of a dimensional regulation.

The error cultivated by the Marxists consists in wishing to impose identical structures from top to bottom of the economic apparatus, from the central hydroelectric plant to the corner dairy shop, from the steel works to the cobbler, from the coal mine to the street vendor.

On the other hand, we cannot admit the wish of the liberal capitalists to leave in the hands of private persons the means of colossal production, which unfailingly end up corrupting and dominating the political power.

The dimension of the enterprise is one of the factors which will determine the organizational system to be applied to it. A private enterprise employing 50,000 workers constitutes a state within a state; the nationalization of an enterprise of 50 workers can only render it sterile.

By specific organization we mean **the character** of the enterprise (manufacture of steel or sale of caramel); by dimensional regulation we understand **the volume** of the latter (50 or 50,000 workers).

51. FROM EXPLOITERS TO ORGANISERS: LET US REALISE THE ECONOMY OF THE UTOPISTS

The excesses of capitalist liberalism have led to concentrations of wealth not with a view to pure political power or some elevated goal but solely with a view to the lowest materialistic enjoyment. Ignoring the national solidarity, the finance capitalist has exploited, without even being aware of his guilt, men of his nation or of other nations. A society where profit is considered as a virtue and a goal must lead fatally to the exploitation of the majority of producers.

This society which has for sole goal material enjoyment and individual wealth we reject before we destroy it. The reign of morally spineless exploiters must cease. The rejection of this capitalist system of exploitation must not lead, through a sort of compensatory rancour, to attempts to realise utopias.

Socialism must be realized with men such as they are and not such as one wishes them to be.

The Communist utopia, derived from the Marxist prophetism and from the proletarian Messianism has caused that, in forty years, this religion has killed more men than any other in the course of history. Reality resisting theory, one has broken men in order to verify miserabilist postulates. In vain.

Nevertheless, in spite of a striking economic failure, Communism remains a powerful myth, an intense hope for those who are crushed by the egoism of capitalist society.

Communism as a socio-economic reality is a spectacular mistake: in order to withdraw from it, it must copy the most elementary and the most banal structures of classical society to which is claims to be superior – but, as a myth to which desperadoes cling and as a means of moral subversion in which the inverted intellectuals wallow, it remains formidable.

It will have taken more than half a century of industrialised cruelties and murders to discover Columbus' egg.[23]

To reject the Golden Calf for Utopia is the aberrant attitude of those who wish to substitute Communism in place of capitalism.

It is up to Europe to realise a utopian economics, that is to say, the economics of dogmatic, bookish Communism.

Communism in its recent revisionist forms tends towards communitarian socialism. It will reach that in some decades after having killed millions of men and devoured thousands of its leaders.

Europe that is the most advanced, the most mature, nation will thus implement the economics of Communist utopia. From exploitative capitalism it will pass directly to communitarian socialism, that is to say, to scientific socialism.

---

[23] 'Columbus' egg' is an expression used to denote any important idea that should, on account of its simplicity, have been discovered earlier than it was.

This communitarian socialism will be thought out and realized by organisers knowing, on the one hand, the human possibilities and their limits and, on the other hand, the transcendent goals of the human species. National communitarian Europe will drive out the exploiters, scatter the utopists and will bring in organisers.

52. EUROPE: THE MINIMUM DIMENSION FOR A SOCIALIST PLANNING

It is useless to attempt a free economy on a small scale; it is much more so to aim at a planned economy in nations of small dimensions.

The smaller a country is the more rapidly the attempt comes up against external obstacles: sources of foreign provision supplies, anarchy of world markets.

Just as for autarky there is for planning a critical value and a volume below which the attempt is destined to failure.

As a hypothesis, a socialist France could not survive in a world divided into advanced industrial economies (the USA, Germany, Japan), impoverished (underdeveloped) economies and Communist economies (dumpings of a political character).

Its suppliers and its clients not being 'socialists' would exercise a determining influence on its style of economico-social organization.

Still as a hypothesis, this attempt of socialist France would have to choose between the maintenance of socialism at the price of an isolation which would make it increasingly lag behind other nations or the abandonment of socialism.

But if a country of the dimension of France depends on overseas sources for 90% of its productive activity, a country like Europe depends, at the present stage, for only 20% – and tomorrow could depend for only 5%.

The problem of dependence is one of inverse proportion. The single man is dependent 100% on others; a nation of 400 million is that not more than 20%.

Thus a small nation cannot freely choose its style of economic and social life, it must take into account multiple foreign interferences. **We state that the smaller a nation is the more it is subject to foreign influences**.

The independence of small nations is nonexistent and fundamentally impossible.

The socialist pseudo-states of small dimensions, Cuba, Algeria, Indonesia, exist only through extortion and through international mendacity. They have left the liberal capitalist tutelage to fall into the Communist tutelage.

No attempt of communitarian socialism is viable below the European dimension. The dimension of the state determines the possibility and the viability of the implementation of a new socio-economic experiment. The socialism of small states is as ridiculous as their will to power.

Each individual, each citizen of a large state is freer than the citizen, or individual, of a small state. In a large nation the citizen participates in freedom and in power, in a small nation the citizen endures dependence and sharing.

Freedom is power. Power is dimension. It is true of nations as of men: only the big ones are really free. Only a large nation like Europe can choose the path of communitarian socialism and maintain itself in it.

53. ACCESS TO RAW MATERIALS, ONE OF THE KEYS OF POLITICAL INDEPENDENCE

Without economic independence there is no true socialism possible.

Economic independence depends in the first place on a free access to raw materials. The finest theoretical construction of a socialist state will collapse if the latter is incapable of accessing alone and freely the sources of raw materials everywhere in the world.

If this state really wishes to live and survive, it must guard its autonomy in this specific sector. Only a strong state offer the means to that.

It is illusory to plan or to socialize any economy which would depend, in the first place, on sources controlled by one or some foreign capitalist powers.

The true socialism—the European national communitarianism—will come via the total liberation of the supplies at present controlled by American capitalism.

The social pretensions of our parliamentarian politicians are of a Platonic socialism: they depend on the American power. The finest plans emerging from the imagination of our politicians are dependent on the costs of raw materials fixed by Finance, on Wall Street.

A stock-exchange coup in New York can provoke the closure of hundred factories in Europe. A government which would really attempt to detach itself from the American tutelage will find itself cut off from its overseas supplies.

We should therefore reconquer the access to and control of several sources of raw materials. It is only when we have realized this objective that we will be really independent.

54. AGAINST INTERNATIONAL MISERABILISM AND A MENDICANT ECONOMY

It is instructive to note that in Europe the most ardent propagandists of aid to the underdeveloped are, on the one hand, the Communists and, on the other, the pro-American underworld. The first wish to empty Europe of its strengths and give it, in addition, guilt-complexes, the second count on deriving substantial profits from it.

The American capitalist societies which plunder our former colonies find it profitable to maintain the native politicians through the finances of the European powers under the disguise of aid.

Some European capitalists have, for their part, found it ingenious to enrich themselves through this 'aid' to the underdeveloped. The aid is, originally, constituted of the taxes received in Europe from our producers. These taxes go to Africa as 'aid'. They are divided, half to the Black politicians and half to the colonial companies in the form of subsidies. The funds granted to the Black politicians are partly accumulated in the banks of neutral countries in very private accounts. When we grant a direct loan to an underdeveloped country it hastens to buy arms in Communist countries!

All these considerations lead us to say that this financial haemorrhage does not improve the condition of the underdeveloped peoples at all, it only fattens their politicians and the international capitalists. These wasted billions are subtracted from the development of our industries in Europe and from the improvement of the salary conditions of our producers.

We must therefore put an end to this waste. The aid to the underdeveloped countries must take another form, adopt other methods.

The European national-communitarian state will put an end to it.

55. AGAINST THE IMPORTATION OF AN EXTRA-EUROPEAN PROLETARIAT

The national-communitarian state will be opposed to the introduction into Europe of extra-European labour formed in very large part of coloured people (North Africa, etc.)

The first reason is that an importation of coloured labour entails a rupture of the ethnic homogeneity of Europe. This argument should suffice, but there are others.

Communism, in western Europe, does not succeed in penetrating deeply into the working producers, men of good sense. Communism registers its only successes in a field less resistant to mental perversion: that of the 'intellectuals'.

Faced with this state of affairs, Communism seeks therefore to introduce among us a more miserable, more nomadic, more unassimilable human category: the coloured people of Africa and elsewhere.

All these coloured people constitute a remarkable mass to be manipulated for the Communist parties. This is the second reason to refuse to introduce them into Europe.

The third reason is that the employers use this socially uneducated and politically unorganized labour force to put pressure on the salaries of the European workers, through a blackmail.

The fourth reason for our opposition resides in the fact that the importation of a cheap labour force allows several badly organized industrial sectors to survive and be parasitical.

An industry which cannot pay high salaries is a badly organized industry. One should prevent the survival of bad sectors.

The fifth reason is that, tomorrow, automation will render unqualified labour useless. Then what will we do with our coloured people? Perpetually unemployed, living at our expense?

All that justifies fully the refusal to introduce non-Europeans into Europe. Those who are there will be repatriated to their respective countries.

56. PUBLIC DISCLOSURE OF WEALTH AND TAXES

In the capitalist-bourgeois societies, profit often comes from speculation or corruption. It goes without saying that the beneficiaries of these immoral profits refuse public disclosure of their resources. It goes without saying also that the politicians who live on this corruption will prevent all legislation destined to throw light on their fiddling.

In a communitarian society, the citizen who would refuse to the official public disclosure of his wealth, his resources, his taxes, would admit thereby a bad conscience.

The national-communitarian state considers that, if legitimate profit can crown personal effort, the society should at the same time be able to track down illicit wealth of fraudulent origin.

Not only the least communal administration, institution of public order, will have to give the most public disclosure to its management but every commercial enterprise and every individual will be bound to render public the principal elements of their circumstances.

Through this self-policing of the society frauds, swindles, embezzlements, evasions of capital will be foreseen, if not prevented. The trade union members will finally know what is done with their contributions. Each isolated but vigilant citizen will be in reality or potentially the controller of the morality of the community.

57. SELF-MANAGEMENT OF SOCIAL INSTRUMENTS

It is necessary to restitute not to the private sector, as the sharks of the insurance companies wish, **but to the cooperative sector, the present social instruments in the fields of accident, unemployment and sickness.** Here as elsewhere it is necessary that there be responsibility on the one hand and competence on the other.

Social security should be denationalized and become cooperative. Doing this, the gifted individuals will be able to detach themselves from the mass and undertake there an apprenticeship of the exercise of power.

The state cannot scatter itself in these activities. The state should remain political, that is to say, superior and an uncontested arbiter. The state should concern itself with a few essential things. The control of the social instruments by the cooperative sector will avoid the state's diluting an energy that it will be able to devote to other tasks.

Not being engaged in management, as it is today, the state will become once again the arbiter, that which it should not have ceased to be.

The present anonymous wastage will be substituted with direct responsible management.

58. THE STATE SHOULD TAKE CARE TO MAINTAIN COMPETITION

The state should take attentive care to see that the competitive mechanisms are never falsified or suffocated by any monopoly.

The tendency of big capitalism is to ensure for itself large and easier profits by suppressing competition through the game of monopolies, or even by eliminating them through protectionist regulations solicited from the state.

The European communitarian state will practise economic nationalism; that means total competitive freedom **within** a **very large** market, a market of more than 400 million men.

One who says rivalry means competition and one who practices competition is assured of the promotion of the best.

59. DEFECTS OF THE COLLECTIVE DECISION

Everybody knows and admits that personal decision entails personal recompense or punishment.

The notion of consequence, favorable or unfavorable, is intimately linked to that of individual decision. That is a healthy conception.

It is different when it is a matter of collective decision. The mediocre, weak or crafty man prefers collective decision because that latter never results in serious negative consequences.

The degeneration of our western bourgeois political system and of the Communist economic system resides in the practice of the evasion of responsibilities through the artifice of a majority decision.

One has never shot members of parliament who had found a majority to declare a stupid war, one has never hanged incompetent people who had wasted billions of hours of work through idiotic economic arrangements, idiotic but 'voted for'?

A system where failure is not punished runs the risk of wastage first, of negligence afterwards, and finally of being surpassed by another nation.

The communitarian system will be based on accentuated responsibility. No majority or ideological immunity will be able to cover idiotic or criminal actions.

At each level of the management the power will be specified, personalized and responsible.

60. DIRIGISME AND CORPORATISM CAN SUFFOCATE AND THEN RUIN A NATION

An invasive and interfering dirigisme, a jealous and narrow corporatism, can make a society anemic and destroy a nation. Parliamentary plutocracy attempts to prolong its agony by the construction of a dense network of regulations which claim to be some social, others professional. In fact, through these practices, it weakens the nation by discouraging the men capable of initiative, when it does not penalize them. The social-bureaucratic ideal of the western politicians is not new, it is constituted of envy, jealousy against the strong, and it often wishes to substitute a society that is often unjust with a mediocre society. The Late Roman Empire became ossified in economico-social regulations, and then collapsed.

The failure of systematic dirigisme has been recently illustrated in all the Communist countries.

A production quantitatively too weak, a production qualitatively mediocre.

The national-communitarian state in its realism will intervene as little as possible in the economic life and, when it does it, it will be with vigour and in the political interest alone.

Dirigisme must constitute the corrective to the egoist or anarchic tendencies possible in certain social functions; it cannot be an end in itself. The impetus of profit remains far superior to coercive methods. The role of the state is to see that this impetus of just retribution differentiated according to effort is never in contradiction to its power.

61. FOR A SINGLE EUROPEAN CURRENCY

The economic power of Europe should stop subsidizing American politics.

The United States of America, which was our creditor in 1945 now finds itself, twenty years later, our debtor.

Nevertheless, the subservience of our politicians to Washington makes us pay, from our own means, a policy that is not ours. NATO is an instrument controlled by the United States but very largely subsidized by the European financial resources.

European money should serve to finance European politics, which is the same as saying, to finance the European army.

It is inadmissible to make the European monetary system gravitate around the dollar, so much more that the latter is losing its substance. In fact, for some years now, it is the French and German monies that have been the strong currencies. **The European economic life should not depend on a foreign currency**. It would have been absurd to see England of the 19th century have as its currency the Italian lira or France of the Third Republic have the mark as its monetary symbol.

We find ourselves at this moment in the paradoxical situation of having a foreign symbol as a monetary standard. The eviction of the American protectorate is via the suppression of the tutelage of the dollar and the creation of a single European currency based on our prodigious economic power.

But it would not be more appropriate to found this single European currency on a gold-standard. In fact, the sources of this metal are essentially outside Europe. To adopt this standard would be to make us fall from one subjection to another.

One must in fact start from the fundamental and imperishable wealth of Europe: its scientific genius, its immense industrial potential, the high qualification of its workers, to create the only standard of value that can liberate us from all tutelage and radically transform the social relations: the work-standard.

62. THE AMERICAN POLITICAL PROTECTORATE IS IMPOSED ON US THROUGH THE INFILTRATION OF AMERICAN FINANCE INTO THE EUROPEAN PLUTOCRACY

The control of the European industries by American finance leads in a direct line to political protectionism.

In western Europe, for several decades, plutocracy reigns disguised as parliamentary democracy. The money powers draw the strings of the political dramas.

For some years we have been witnessing the progressive gangrene of the European plutocracy through American high finance.

The European politician personages being subject to the European plutocracy and the latter becoming increasingly subordinated to American finance, it follows that **European politics finds itself progressively controlled by extra-European forces**.

The reconquest of European political freedom will be through the repurchase of all the American economic positions here and, in case of contestation or resistance, through their confiscation pure and simple, to the profit of the nation.

63. NATIONALISATION OF AMERICAN ASSETS

The existence of very important American—thus foreign—financial participations in our economy constitutes a violation of our political independence. Through financial intervention a foreign nation can slow down the industrial expansion, plunder our work, and through a neo-colonial capitalist economics provoke social crises, disorganize the military industry, corrupt the power. A powerful state does not tolerate any interference. Therefore the national-communitarian state will repurchase all the American assets at their intrinsic—and not speculative—value.

In the accounting of this repurchase will be counted the just reparation of the thefts committed by the United States for 25 years, in the extortions and pillages from Indonesia to Katanga,[24] by way of Algeria.

The least inimical act with regard to Unitarian Europe will entail this time the confiscation of

---

[24] Katanga is one of the richest provinces of the former Belgian Congo and present Democratic Republic of the Congo. Under Moise Tshombe it broke away in 1960 from the Republic of Congo-Léopoldville which was established when the Belgian Congo became independent of Belgium. Tshombe's breakaway state was considered a Belgian-controlled puppet state. However, Tshombe surrendered to UN forces in 1962.

the American assets without any compensation whatsoever.

These foreign assets recuperated by the European state will be resold to the European collectivities.

X – THE GOAL

64. PREPARING THE MERGING OF THE ECONOMIES OF OUR EASTERN PROVINCES WITH OUR WESTERN PROVINCES

The political reunification of Europe will be notably conditioned by the economico-social structures of its two temporarily separated parts.

A western Europe of an archaic capitalist style dominated by American finance and an eastern Europe of dogmatic Marxist style plundered by Russia makes the political reunification of our great fatherland very difficult.

Thus we should foresee in the west the establishment of communitarian structures, that is to say, free enterprise of a disciplined, national and social sort.

The presence of American finance capitalism in Europe makes this reform impossible. That is why the first task of Communitarianism will be the expropriation of all the American interests in Europe.

We denounce a certain 'West', a Yankee economic empire that extends from Frankfurt to Tokyo, dominated by the Carthaginians of Manhattan, and whose interests are opposed to ours.

The reunification of Europe will be facilitated if, in the east, our temporarily Communist provinces abandon the Marxist dogmatism to slide towards a realistic reformism and if, in the west, we replace the capitalist financial structures with Communitarianism.

In the east, the enterprises will be denationalized and made cooperative; in the west the enterprises will be de-Americanised and made progressively Communitarian.

Plutocratic western Europe – rightly – makes the peoples of our eastern provinces distrustful.

But a national-communitarian western Europe will constitute an irresistible magnet for them.

The establishment of communitarian socialism in western Europe will motivate the reformist Communist leaders of our eastern provinces – under the pressure of their base – to pass into our camp with arms and baggage and to turn against the Russian occupier. That is not possible as long as we tolerate the American army in Bavaria and the sharks of Wall Street in Frankfurt.

65. COMMUNITARIANISM

Communitarianism is a secular socialism, detached from utopias, purged of dogmas, freed from stereotypes.

Communitarianism is the national fact inseparable from the social, the realistic perception that socialism cannot be accomplished outside the protective habitat of a nation and that a nation cannot be divorced from its people.

Communitarianism is a scientific socialism; it knows that one cannot suffocate creative initiative; it knows the vigour of free enterprise and its utility for the nation. A strong nation maintains enterprise within its limits and prevents it from degenerating into speculative and exploitative finance capitalism.

Western socialism has degenerated because it has attempted to deny the national reality and tried to realise an abstract socialism as a mythical ecumenism.

In its parliamentary forms it is corrupted fully. It is today the alibi for the most ignoble plutocracy.

Everywhere in western Europe parliamentary socialism has removed itself from the European nation by organizing a hypocritical symbiosis with capitalism, by being the rump party of the clan of the American occupier.

The more violent, more dogmatic socialism has organized an economic disarray for half a century by postulating an economy starting from theoretical considerations of Marx. It has attempted to endorse its mistakes through an opposition created expressly for this purpose. The facts being resistant to theory, Communism, in its dogmatic rancor, has assassinated millions of men.

In half a century Communism will end, whether it likes it or not, in Communitarianism. But after having filled up cemeteries, Europe, an advanced nation, must avoid this bloody utopia.

Communitarianism is essentially pragmatist; it wishes to tend towards a better, more accomplished, more developed, man, but it knows that it must do that with men as they are.

Communitarianism – a perfect balance between the security needs and the libertarian demands of man – refuses the permanent reign of bureaucracy, religion or the proletariat.

Irresponsibility and demagogy will be opposed by Communitarianism with the permanent mutual responsibility of everyone and with a hierarchy based on values not on privileges.